Portrait of Prague

Portrait of Prague

PHOTOGRAPHED BY K. NEUBERT AND A. SRCH

TEXT BY EMANUEL POCHE

PAUL HAMLYN

LONDON · NEW YORK · SYDNEY · TORONTO

Translated by John Eisler

Graphic design by Zdeněk Rossmann

Designed and produced by Artia

Published 1969 by

THE HAMLYN PUBLISHING GROUP LIMITED
LONDON • NEW YORK • SYDNEY • TORONTO

Hamlyn House, Feltham, Middlesex, England

Text © 1969 by Emanuel Poche

Illustrations © 1969 Nos. 1—10, 12—15, 17—21, 23, 24, 26—29, 32, 33, 35, 36, 40—42, 44—56, 58—66, 68—75, 77, 83—87, jacket and frontispiece by Karel Neubert, Nos. 11, 16, 22, 25, 30, 31, 34, 37—39, 43, 57, 67, 76, 78—82 by Antonín Srch

Printed in Czechoslovakia by Svoboda, Prague
S 2304

Prague is a synthesis of natural beauty and human creativeness. The contours of the land, eroded as they have been for thousands of years by the waters of the Vltava, in themselves provide attractive scenery. The steep slopes of the river's left bank — Letná Hill, Hradčany Hill, the Prague Castle, and Petřín Hill, covered with dense greenery — within whose circular wedge lies the picturesque amphitheatre of the Little Quarter, form a contrast to the wide flat area on the right bank, behind which rise Vítkov Hill and the Vinohrady Quarter at one end and Karlov and Vyšehrad at the other. It was between these, at the bend of the Vltava and more than a thousand years ago, that the core of present-day Prague came into existence. Here, at a shallow ford, foreign merchants and traders began to settle, newcomers from both the south and the east. To these came the inhabitants of the surrounding heights, where at Bubeneč and, later, on Hradčany Hill lay the first historically documented hamlets within the area of today's city, to exchange and barter goods. The foreigners brought rare plants and other products, and in exchange the local inhabitants offered them food, furs, leather goods, the chance of comfortable rest, and also protection on the next stage of their travels.

These local peoples were subordinated at the beginning of the ninth century to a tribe known as the Czechs. Led by the Přemyslid family, they later stabilized both the settlement of the amalgamated tribes and their trade relationships by founding two fortified areas, the earlier one in the second half of the ninth century on Hradčany Hill, and the later, about the middle of the tenth century, on Vyšehrad. In this way a new administrative, economic and cultural centre began to develop. It was called *Praha* (Prague), and with the rising power of the Přemyslid princes, it acquired more and more importance.

At first Prague was a conglomeration of villages, the most significant of which was the colony of Jewish immigrants, in view of their trading skills and attendant prosperity. The oldest recorded mention of Prague is that of the Arab writer Al Bekri of Córdoba, and it is based on a report by the Jewish merchant Ibrahim Ibn Jacob, a member of a Moorish deputation to the Emperor Otto I. At that time, about the year 965, Ibn Jacob visited Prague and is alleged to have recalled it in the following terms: 'Prague is the centre of lively trade in Bohemia. To it come Russians, Poles, Mohammedans, Jews and Hungarians to buy slaves, tin, furs, riding saddles, harnesses and shields, in fact everything that is produced there. Prague is a town built of stone and lime.'

In this respect the much travelled merchant exaggerated. According to archaeological finds this statement could only refer to the prince's castle complex. Here, in fact from as early as about 890, stood a stone Church of the Virgin Mary, the first Christian sanctuary in Bohemia, founded by the first historically known prince of Bohemia, Bořivoj. Apart from this there was the stone Basilica of

St George, built by Prince Vratislav in about 921, and a third stone building, the Rotunda of St Vitus, built by Prince Václav (Wenceslas) about ten years later, only to become, almost immediately, his burial place. This ruler, who by his martyrdom became the first saint of his people, became also the patron saint of Bohemia.

This was surely all the lime and stone the traveller from Spain could have seen; all the other buildings of the castle complex, including the prince's palace and, over a wider area, the buildings of the outer bailey and surrounding hamlets, were made of mud and wood, and the same materials were used for the fortifications of the prince's castle.

It was the same at Vyšehrad, which is first mentioned at the time of Boleslav II. This prince was not only a devout Christian, but also a good politician and a man of culture. By founding the bishopric of the Church of St Vitus in 973 he freed his country from dependence on the bishop of Regensburg. By establishing a convent of the Benedictine nuns beside the Church of St George in 973, and the men's Benedictine monastery in Břevnov on the outskirts of Prague in 993, he contributed significantly to the spiritual and cultural elevation of his territory.

The next important cultural enrichment of Prague did not come till about a hundred years later, at the time of Vratislav II, the first king of Bohemia. For a time he transferred the prince's residence to Vyšehrad and proceeded to endow this fortress handsomely. Here he founded a chapter house and built a stone palace and three churches, of which the Rotunda of St Martin stands to this day. The oldest preserved Czech illuminated manuscript, the *Vyšehrad Evangeliarium*, was painted for his coronation in 1085. It was during his time, also, that a new dominating feature of Prague originated, namely the Basilica of St Vitus, on the site of the former Rotunda of St Wenceslas. As recorded by the chronicler Cosmas, Prague at that time flowed with gold and silver, and was a place rich above others in commerce. Trade, at that period, was concentrated on a wide market place which can be identified with today's Old Town Square. It was also at about that time that a hospice and chapel for foreign traders were built, together with the prince's customs' house, known as the Ungelt. Stone houses for the merchants began to rise around the market place, and this activity came to its climax during the reign of Vladislav II (1140—73).

Vladislav was an ally of Frederick Barbarossa. This alliance brought Vladislav not only a king's crown but also immense military spoils. From this and from trading profits, which, by then, were already substantially provided by German merchants for whom an independent colony had been established on Poříč, late Romanesque Prague developed both architecturally and culturally. The castle compound was transformed into a Romanesque palace, above which rose not only the towers of the Basilica of St Vitus but also the new Basilica of St George, which was rebuilt in its present form after the fire of 1142. The two baileys of the Castle, on the left and right banks of the river, were connected by a new stone bridge more than 500 yards long and named (prior to 1172) in honour of Vladislav's wife, Judith's Bridge. It was the pride od the kingdom and the only stone bridge, apart from the bridges of Regensburg and Würzburg, in central Europe. It was also at that time that three more cloisters came into existence in Prague, including the famous Premonstratensian Monastery at Strahov.

And so, at the turn of the thirteenth century, Prague figures as one of the largest towns of the time, numbering some fifty churches and a large quantity of stone patrician houses, more than a hundred remains of which have been discovered beneath the foundations of present-day houses in Prague's Old Town. Not only did trade thrive in this splendid town, but the same was noticeable in the arts and in spiritual life. Documentary records of the creative arts of this period are scarce, but from written reports we learn a lot about widely spread activities in the fields of painting, sculpture and handicrafts, in particular in casting and enamelling, and, above all, in the embroidery of ecclesiastical vestments, which was done at home by gentlewomen. Minting and medallion-making were also of great importance.

Towards the end of the Romanesque period Prague had all the material and cultural prerequisites for becoming a legally constituted town. This development occurred during the reign of King Václav I, in about 1230. At that time the outer bailey surrounding the large market place, together with the new market and colony around the newly founded Church of St Gall, were fortified with walls, and the inhabitants were granted the rights and freedoms of town citizens. Thus is was that the Old Town of Prague came into existence. The outer bailey beneath the castle itself, on the opposite bank of the river, was fortified during the reign of Přemysl II, in 1257, and was named the Lesser Town of Prague. It was otherwise known as the Little Quarter, and its population acquired rights modelled on those of Magdeburg. As a result of the granting of rights and special privileges to the rich citizens by the king, the wealth of the towns of Prague increased and class differences became more pronounced.

The transformation of Prague into a town in legal terms also opened the gates to Gothic art and, with it, to new forms of spiritual and secular life. The instigators and supporters of Gothic spiritual culture were the mendicant monastic orders, the Franciscans and Dominicans, whose residences in the town also introduced various evolutionary stages of European Gothic architecture.

The growing trade relations and political expansion of Přemysl II, who was known as 'the iron and gold king', found expression in the secular way of life of the ruling classes, the aristocracy and the patriciate of that time. Czech nobles now came into direct contact with western culture. Prague society's way of life and dress was now dominated by the customs of the knights of chivalry. Hunting and tournaments filled the gentry's free time, and the import of silk from Italy and cloth from the Netherlands brought luxury into clothing. The high cultural demands of Přemysl are reflected not only in his rebuilding of the Romanesque castle into a Gothic one, but also in his contacts with the Arab astronomers and astrologists who visited Prague during his reign.

Přemysl's cultural leanings were also shared by his son, Václav II, who gave expression to them by preparing the ground for the founding of a university; but this came to nought owing to the opposition of the aristocracy and the premature death of the king.

And so the task of turning Prague into a university town was left to his grandson, Charles IV, the issue of John of Luxembourg and Václav's daughter, Eliška, the last of the Přemyslid family. From her Charles inherited cultural ambitions which acquired substance and refinement during a lengthy stay, as a very young man, at the French court, where he later became engaged to Blanche de Valois, the sister of King Philip VI. Charles was strongly attached to Prague and gave to her the major part of his political, material and cultural acquisitions. To this day, at every step, one comes across monuments and buildings connected with this sovereign, who was the first Czech king to become Holy Roman Emperor and thus made Prague the capital of the Holy Roman Empire.

Immediately following his return from France he had the palace of the Prague Castle rebuilt in a form similar to the palaces of the French kings. In 1344, in connection with the elevating of the bishopric of Prague to an archbishopric, Charles had the Romanesque Basilica of St Vitus pulled down and started building a Gothic cathedral, the plans for which were devised by Matthew of Arras and, after the latter's premature death, by Peter Parler. Prague University was founded in 1348, the fourth in Europe after those of Paris, Padua and Bologna. The cultural undertakings of Charles constitute a continuous chain of well considered intentions. The raising of Prague to the status of an archbishopric brought about the building of the Gothic cathedral; the founding of the university, in its turn, was the origin of another magnificent project, namely the founding of the New Town of Prague. This achievement was not only a legal act but, as can be seen to this day from its ground-plans and panoramic views, also a well thought-out urban concept that stands up favourably even when seen against modern planning techniques.

The reason behind the founding of the New Town was the idea that the colleges of the new university, situated as they were in the Old Town, were to be freed from the noise caused by the trades and handicrafts which had been carried on in that part of the town until then. Needless to say, this was only a pretext for the emperor to be able to carry out his plan for an ideal city, monolithic in its ground-plan and in the structure of its buildings on the perimeter of the Old Town. The layout of the New Town was kept strictly to a system of streets symmetrically arranged in relation to the three market places. Likewise the individual houses, whose construction was made possible by tax reliefs, were also designed according to an exact plan governing area and height. At all the focal points of the New Town the emperor had churches and cloisters founded, which towered high above the otherwise low roof-level of the dwelling houses, and together with their adjoining gardens and cemeteries, created green islands among the grey buildings of the town. These churches represent a collection of all the then extant types of sacred buildings.

The spiritual orders that Charles allowed to settle there also reflected the complex assembly of contemporary religious orders. Of these the most remarkable were the Slavonic Benedictines in the Emmaus cloister, who were given permission by the Pope to hold services in the old Slavonic language. This cloister is noticeable, also, for its place in the evolution of the architecture of Prague; but, above all, it is the paintings in the ambit that were of foremost importance in the development of late Gothic wall-painting in Bohemia.

Charles's mania for collecting, which evinced itself mainly in the collecting of saints' relics, goldsmith ware and illuminated manuscripts, served in the first place to enrich the treasure of the Cathedral of St Vitus, kept at that time in the Chapel of St Wenceslas. Saints' relics were added to this treasure almost yearly, from both the empire and kingdom, and in this way Prague gradually became a place of pilgrimage for the whole of Europe. She also became a real European town, not only in the political but even in the cultural sense. And so here, where there already existed water mains and paved streets, where the streets were cleaned and where beyond the new fortifications there were acres of vineyards founded by Charles IV himself, there was now a flowering of the arts, sciences and music. It was here that the style known as 'the beautiful style', the Czech school of painting and sculpture, originated and attracted deputations and individuals from abroad. They brought with them a knowledge of foreign customs, social life, manners, fashion and the culture of living.

The words of Petrarch, in a letter to Archbishop Arnošt of Pardubice, after his visit to Prague, prove better than anything else the cultural achievements of imperial Prague at that time:

'I own that nowhere and never have I seen anyone so
cultured as the Emperor and the various illustrious
men around him, men of prominence and deserving of
the highest praise, such as could have been
born citizens of Athens in Athens.'

At the end of the reign of Charles IV (died 1378) Prague was the third largest city in Europe after Rome and Constantinople, and in number of inhabitants (40,000) second only to Rome.

In the following forty years building and cultural activities reached their climax in this 'garden of delight' *(hortus deliciarum)* as Prague was described by Charles IV. Fortunately Charles' son, Václav IV, inherited his father's cultural interests and, though a failure politically, he had great feeling for his home town and took pains with the carrying out and completion of its construction. He took an active part in the endeavours then being made to achieve a moral rebirth of mankind, which brought him into conflict with immoral and dogmatic clergy. In order to be closer to his people he left the castle and set up his Court in the Old Town, where he established a library of manuscripts which were adorned by a whole series of outstanding illuminators. Their work can be admired today mainly in the National Library in Vienna.

He was well disposed towards the University and presented it with a house (the present Carolinum); he showed special friendship towards the rector, John Huss, who at that time used to preach in the newly built Bethlehem Chapel against the immorality of the Church and appeal to the people to strive for a change in social and national conditions. During Václav's reign, Prague became the focal point of the revolutionary Hussite movement. The king did not live to see more than its initial stages, but it was his sympathy that inflamed the fires which consumed almost the entire land and brought it into warlike conflict with the whole of contemporary Europe. It was at that time that Prague lost its position as capital of the empire, but on the other hand it became a bastion of the strivings for a moral and religious rebirth, for a return to the simple teachings of Christ.

In the course of this conflict the might of the king collapsed and power was transferred to the Czech Utraquist stratum of merchants and craftsmen, which had become rich from the confiscated property of the Church and the exiled German patriciate. This stratum then became the bearer not only of the main political and economic activity, but also of further enterprise in the city.

The cultural aspirations of these burghers, understandably enough, began to be expressed in the rebuilding of the Town Halls of both the Old and New Towns of Prague, and in the building of the Old Town Gate, which is today known as the Powder Tower. The construction of this tower was commenced in 1475 by the gifted and sensitive builder, Matěj Rejsek. At the same period Rejsek also enhanced the architecture of Prague's astronomical Clock Tower, the mechanism of which was improved, about the year 1490, by Master Hanuš. The private houses of the burghers were by now filled with luxury goods; costly silks were imported from Italy, and Venetian glass and mirrors competed with the home-produced ware of silver and tin. 'The Czech society is corrupted by luxury', wrote one of the first Czech humanists, Bohuslav of Lobkovicz.

The cultural awareness of the burghers was beginning to be influenced by book printing which became an industrial undertaking in Prague in 1487. The power and political demands of the citizens, emanating from their commerce and trade, finally came into open conflict with the powers of the king, the weak Vladislav Jagello, who ascended the throne after Jiří of Poděbrady — known, incidentally, as the author of the first famous peace manifesto. In 1483 Vladislav had to flee before the uprising of his Utraquist subjects, leaving the Royal Court in the Old Town for the safety of the Prague Castle. This was not without profit to the Castle buildings. Thanks to the king's appreciation of culture, building and artistic activity came again to the Castle, led, at first, by Hans Spiess of Frankfurt and then, after 1489, by Benedikt Rejt of Pístov. To him goes the credit for the unique Vladislav Hall, in which he happily blended late Gothic vaulting with Renaissance windows. The Hall was used for tournaments, for meetings of the representatives of the Estates, for Court sittings and royal banquets. The oldest depiction of Prague, published in the Schedel Chronicle, dates from this period.

It was only when the strong man, Ferdinand Habsburg, ascended the Czech throne in 1526, that the rights (but not the cultural endeavours) of the citizens were drastically restricted. In spite of the antagonism of the aristocracy, the citizens continued with the building of Prague in the spirit of South European culture which had been brought to Prague by the king and his court. It was at this point that Italian Renaissance took root in Prague on a large scale. The town became an eldorado for Italian builders, who founded their own dwelling quarter in the Little Quarter and, prior to 1540, on behalf of the emperor started work on the building of the Royal Summer-House, as a part of the first architecturally designed garden in Bohemia. Not only tournaments but also ball-games and theatre performances took place in this cultured setting, which was so pervaded by the spirit of the Renaissance. The nobility created a truly regal court here. At the Castle and in its close environment splendid palaces arose, combining Italian Renaissance with local building practice. The noble families, such as the Rožmberks, Pernštejns, Lobkoviczs, Griespeks, the lords of Hradec, and others, together with the king, thus left their mark on the Renaissance construction of Prague after 1550, both in the materials used and in the form and decoration of façades — and the lower aristocracy followed their example in the outer bailey of the Castle.

The townspeople who, in spite of political oppression, still had sufficient money, now built themselves new family houses, or at least applied Renaissance decor to older buildings. Painted beam ceilings and lavish interiors in the palaces and houses, which were being filled with Italian furniture, enamelled beer cups, Italian and home-made majolica, along with grave-stones decorated with figures and epitaphs, and the illuminated hymn-books of the literary brotherhoods, are characteristic of Renaissance Prague. At that time Prague also experienced its first public theatre performance, which was given by the Jesuits shortly after 1556 as a means of propagating the counter-reformation. In the accoutrements of a burgher's family of that day, side by side with foreign literature, one also comes across books from Prague printing houses with hand-worked bindings made by outstanding Prague book-binders; there were also private picture galleries.

After 1573 Rudolf II again turned Prague Castle into a residence. Like Charles IV earlier,

Rudolf also suffered from a mania for collecting. He brought together important artists, craftsmen, goldsmiths, clockmakers, mechanics and others. He had a summer palace built, together with a garden known as the Garden of Paradise, another set of stables, the Lion's Court, a grove of fig trees, two assembly halls, and a treasury for rare natural objects, a collection of minerals and a world-famous art collection. To this day the most important museums of the world boast of works from Rudolf's picture gallery which, shortly after his death in 1612, became the victim of the greed of the various powers that occupied Prague and also of his successors to the throne.

Rudolf II was a patron of mechanics and astronomy; he gave hospitality to Tycho de Brahe and Johannes Kepler, and the latter formulated his first two astronomical laws while working in Prague. Rudolf also believed in alchemy, but here his judgement betrayed him and he let himself be fooled by various adventurers. Although he had been brought up at the Spanish court of Philip II, he favoured Protestants, progressive philosophers and Jews. It was at that time that Giordano Bruno and numerous French Huguenots appeared in Prague. His reign was also the golden age of the Prague Jewish ghetto. Philosophy, science and trade flowered. It was there, according to legend, that Rabbi Löw, who was specially favoured by the emperor, made his Golem and magic lantern, and that Mordechai Maizl, who was the emperor's financier, built himself a beautiful Renaissance palace in the ghetto and his fellow believers a new synagogue and Talmud School.

About the year 1600 Prague was a metropolis of sixty thousand inhabitants, a town in which people from all walks of life came together. It was now mainly North European political influences that left their mark upon the face of the town, although one also comes across the first manifestations of Italian Baroque as an indication of the future fate of the town and the whole countryside.

When Rudolf died in 1612, his much-hated brother and successor, Matthias, moved with his entourage to Vienna. He died not long afterwards and his nephew, the bigoted Catholic Ferdinand II, ascended the throne. But even before his coronation the Protestant Czech upper classes rejected him, threw his imperial chancellors from the windows of Prague Castle and elected as king the no less bigoted Calvinist, Frederick the Winter King. Ferdinand collected an army and, in the Battle of the White Mountain on 8 November 1620, succeeded in subjecting the Czech Lands to his rule by force. His revenge fell not only on the leaders of the uprising, of whom twenty-seven were executed in the Old Town Square in June 1621, but also on the whole Czech nation.

Prague sank to the level of an administrative centre of one of the countries of the Habsburg monarchy. The Utraquists were exiled and their property confiscated, those benefiting from this being the Catholics and, above all, the loyal followers of Ferdinand. The horrors of the Thirty Years' War and, mainly, the looting of Hradčany and the Little Quarter by the Swedes in 1648, completed the processes of submission to foreign overlords, the counter-reformation and the revival of rigid feudalism.

The town was depopulated, trade and culture declined. Those who stayed were forced to accept Catholicism and more or less serve the emperor, the foreign aristocracy or the clergy. These, even during the course of the war, had already begun to leave the imprint of their power on Prague. The Baroque palace, cloister or church became the typical marks of their sovereignty. The appearance of the town, its lay-out and form, were more than ever before determined by Italy, thanks to the mass immigration of Italian builders, plasterers and stone-masons. The Wallenstein, Michna, Nosticz and

Czernin palaces and Jesuit convents in the Old Town, New Town and Little Quarter, the cloisters of the Carmelites and others, built in various modes of Italian classicism, seized vast areas of ground from the demolished houses of the townspeople, regardless of their medieval surroundings. Their long horizontal forms, towering high above the neighbouring buildings and the new Italian-style monotone brick ramparts that replaced the picturesque Gothic walls of the town after 1648, all rose like bastions of a foreign power above the subject town.

But at the end of the seventeenth century there came a change. Thanks to a new generation of builders, to much-travelled noblemen both secular and clerical, to the consolidation of the economic conditions in the land, and last but not least, to creative architects, the standard of building activity in Prague rose and Baroque lost its barb of political propaganda and synthesized with the real environment of the town. An indigenous Prague Baroque took shape, first of all in painting — thanks to the renowned portraitist and creator of altar canvases, Karel Škréta — and, later, in other branches of artistic expression. Architectural evolution reached European standards again with the arrival of the Romanized Frenchman, Jean B. Mathey, the designer of the Church of the Knights Hospitalers and the Château at Troja near Prague. We also find here the first grandiose murals, introduced by Abraham Godyn from Antwerp, as well as sculptures, credit for which goes to the Heermans from Dresden. Out of all these stimulating contributions, which were a response to the cultural demands of the Czech nobility and the clergy, by 1710 we find a superb, entirely Czech Baroque developing: Baroque of the Dientzenhofers, of Santini, Kaňka, and leading architects; the sculptural Baroque of Brokoff and Braun; and the monumental paintings of Brandl and Reiner. It was an art that was no longer merely a concoction and second-rate product, but was an expression of an age-old indigenous creativeness which in the sensuality of Baroque found a creative manifestation more akin to itself than anything else. Baroque was an important contribution on the part of the Czech creative spirit to the art treasury of the world, and the unique means of manifesting a politically enslaved spirit. It was not only the fine arts, but also the theatre — for which Count Sporck had the first permanent stage built in 1704 — and Czech music, which in their turn served to enrich European music with the works of Brixi, Černohorský, and many others.

By the end of the first half of the eighteenth century Baroque was triumphant in Prague, and was expressing itself as an entity and in detail, both indoors and out. By the time Maria Theresa had the various buildings on the western side of the Castle rebuilt into a homogenous Baroque palace, between 1756 and 1777, this culmination of the Baroque rebirth of the city was resounding with a mighty fanfare, in which alongside Rococo lyricism the sound of approaching rationalism and still hushed voices of freemasonry were to be heard. The earlier fanatical religiousness was being drowned in a new interest in life: eyes formerly fixed on the heavenly firmament now directed their gaze to earthly reality. Wolfgang Amadeus Mozart became the darling of Prague, to Prague he dedicated his *Don Giovanni*, which received its first performance in the Nosticz (Tyl) Theatre. The lodges of the freemasons were preparing the ground on which the ideas of the French revolutionaries could take root. The ennobled citizenry, which by that time was beginning to compete socially with the upper aristocracy, played a considerable part in all this. But the influence of the nouveau riche bourgeoisie was becoming noticeable in the churches, palaces, ancient patrician houses, gardens and parks, picture galleries and concert halls; they set up manufacturing companies and, later, built factories.

The enlightened monarch Joseph II, with his various reforms, contributed considerably to this metamorphosis. He opened the gates to a new age, the age of the social expansion of the bourgeoisie, with its stringent interest in obtaining political and economic benefits, an aim which was furthered by the first industrial exhibition held in Prague in 1791.

When serfdom was abolished in 1783 Prague became the goal of countless peasants looking for work in the growing number of industrial enterprises. Parallel with this, the self-confidence of the Czech people in terms of nation and language was also rising. The Age of Enlightenment encouraged nationalistic ideas among the people, which quickly gained strength. About the year 1800 the Czech language was seldom heard spoken in the streets of Prague, but by the year 1848 it had become the dominant tongue and, in 1861, a Czech was elected mayor of the city for the first time after an interval of more than 200 years.

The secretive work of the Czech revival that had been carried on by patriotic priests, teachers, writers and poets, now began to reach Prague from the countryside, where it entered into open struggle for a Czech policy and linguistic freedom. The struggle for the creation of a new national culture was directed towards the same ends. In the forefront of this, together with the Czech towns-people, were Czech aristocrats who deserve the credit for founding the Czech Scholars' Society in 1771, the Gallery of Patriotic Friends of Art in 1796, and the Academy of Fine Arts in 1800. The National Museum was founded in 1818, the Conservatoire of Music came into being in 1816, and in 1835 the first public library with reading-room was opened.

On the other hand, the new constructive activities required by the cultural and economic needs of life were insensible to the architectural wealth of Prague's past. The exception to this was the planning of new parks and summer residences on the perimeter of the town. During the first half of the nineteenth century the place of the architect had been taken over by the builder himself, who was more of a technician than an artist, and to whom tasks of a technical or ameliorating nature were more appropriate. For instance, in 1847 the first railway station was built (today's Prague Central); the first swimming-pool in 1830, the first gas-works in 1847, and other similar constructions.

With rare exceptions, the building programme no longer included the building of palaces and churches. Their places had been taken by apartment houses, which were strictly utilitarian and were more or less merely pasted over with the classicist décor that characterized the buildings of the first suburbs beyond the town walls.

The culmination of the new practical renaissance and Czech art of the nineteenth century was the National Theatre, the work of J. Zítek and a whole generation of sculptors and painters, representing the flower of artistic culture of the time.

But the Czech bourgeoisie, which was steadily growing richer and politically stronger, did not limit itself to following the creative trends set by Zítek and his associates, and, as elsewhere, revealed itself outwardly by reducing great art to a mass of pseudo-styles and decorative plastering over of apartment houses, schools, banks and department stores. This practice, which was perhaps almost acceptable in the suburbs, represented a tragedy for the historical kernel of Prague. At the time when the Czech Academy of Arts and Sciences was being founded, when the newly created Applied Arts Museum, Applied Arts School and the new art associations were concerned with elevating public taste and preserving the beauties of the past, the Prague ghetto and the adjoining parts of the Old

Town were being levelled to the ground and the New Town was being pulled down wholesale. On the sites so demolished rose pseudo-style houses, yielding financial profit but being culturally worthless.

A sudden realization of the irreparable damage being done to the city ultimately saved Hradčany, the Little Quarter and a major part of the Old Town from brute speculation. Thanks to this and to the great national exhibitions held at the end of the nineteenth century — such as the Jubilee Exhibition of 1891, the Ethnographic Exhibition and the Exhibition of Architects and Technicians — the wholesale demolition of the city's architectural treasures finally came to an end, and we reach the point where, around 1900, the city was introduced to Art Nouveau and, later, to modern art as propagated by the founder of modern Czech architecture, Jan Kotěra and his school. Alongside the old, historic lly and artistically valuable buildings now appeared comparable architecture which, together with the changing civilization and up-to-date facilities, now served to shape the emerging metropolis.

With the fall of the Austro-Hungarian monarchy in 1918, Prague again became the capital of an independent country. The founding of the Czechoslovak Republic strengthened Prague's role as the centre of the people's culture and offered it further possibilities of development in the fields of literature, music, the fine arts, science and education. The city was enriched by magnificent new public buildings and enlarged by new districts in the north-west sector, of which the residential areas of Baba and Ořechovka represented the culmination of contemporary Czechoslovak town planning and urban construction. In this the constructivist school of Czech architecture achieved international fame.

The Nazi occupation in 1939 interrupted the prosperous evolution of the city, and wartime stagnation continued to be felt even after the end of hostilities in 1945. It was only when the socialist system came into being in 1948 that the cultural life of the city began to revive. A whole series of historically important buildings, starting with Prague Castle, were repaired, and many were adapted to provide new cultural facilities, such as galleries, museums, scientific institutes, and so on. Never before had the State made so many funds available to science, culture and the development of the city as now. Dozens of higher schools of learning, two picture galleries, three full-scale orchestras, ten exhibition halls, thirty theatres, three concert halls, seventy-five cinemas, ten libraries and twenty museums, a Park of Culture and a number of sports facilities give an indication of the cultural level of Prague today.

At the same time, the continuous building of a new Prague goes on in accordance with the growth of the population (1,200,000) and its material and cultural demands and needs. The new city is growing up around the perimeter of the old, thereby respecting tradition and sparing the inheritance of the past thousand years. The leaders and elders of the city are aware that in historic Prague, in its preservation and sensitive inclusion into contemporary life, lies the future of one of the oldest and most beautiful cities of the world.

Emanuel Poche

LIST OF ILLUSTRATIONS

Frontispiece: The Old Town Hall; detail of the horologe which originated around 1410. It was improved towards the end of the 15th century, restored in 1552—60, 1865, 1880—82, and after 1945. The architecture dates from 1410 (the circle) and the end of the 15th century (the consoles and canopies); the sculptures from the second half of the 17th century; the zodiac panel from 1865.

1 A panoramic view of the Vltava river with the New Town weir in the foreground and the Jewish Island on the left. Shooters' (Pioneers') Island and the Bridge of the 1st of May are in the centre, and the Slavonic Island on the right. The first two islands date from the 15th, the third came into existence in the 18th century. In the background on the left are Prague Castle with the Cathedral of St Vitus, dating from the 14th century; on the right is the Old Town with the cupola of the Church of the Knights Hospitalers which dates from the end of the 17th century; at the extreme right is the roof of the National Theatre, dating from 1883—84.

2 Kampa, the island which existed as early as the 12th century by the Little Quarter bank of the river; on the right, Prague Castle with the Cathedral, and Petřín Hill with its lookout tower dating from 1891 on the left.

3 Morning on the Vltava below the Smetana embankment, with a panoramic view of Prague Castle and the Little Quarter. The long frontage of the Castle, spanning the 12th—18th centuries, is crowned by the Cathedral of St Vitus and by the towers of the Church of St George (12th century). The palace rising above the Little Quarter in the foreground, at one time known as the Liechtenstein, and originally as the Kaiserstein Palace, dating from the end of the 17th century, but rebuilt in 1864.

4 Another panoramic view of Prague, from the lookout tower, gives a vivid picture of the layout and evolution of the city. The Vltava splits Prague into two parts: in the foreground, on the left bank, lie Prague Castle and the Little Quarter, beyond the river are the Old and New Towns of Prague. In the background are suburbs dating from the 19th century. Above the Castle is the Letná plateau, where army parades and sports events take place.

5 Prague Castle and the Little Quarter, with Charles Bridge in the foreground. Prague Castle, situated beneath and around the Cathedral of St Vitus, consists of the Old Palace and, to its left, the new Theresian Palace from the 18th century. To its right is the former Institute for Noblewomen, which dates from the middle of the 18th century. To the left of the Castle spreads Hradčany, the outer bailey settlement of the Castle, dating from the 14th—18th centuries. It is enclosed on the left-hand side by the towers of the Strahov Church (18th century), and the former monastery, today the Museum of Czech Literature, from the 12th—18th centuries. The Little Quarter, the most ancient part of Prague, was founded as a town in 1257 and acquired its present form during reconstructions in the 16th and 18th centuries. Charles Bridge was founded in 1357; its sculptures date from 1683—1714.

6 The bridges of Prague with a part of the Old Town. Mánes Bridge (1911—16), is in the foreground; next comes Charles Bridge (second half of the 14th century) with its tower; then the Bridge of the 1st of May, which was built in 1903 in place of an iron bridge dating from 1840, the second bridge to exist in Prague. Behind that are Jirásek Bridge (1936) and, finally, Palacký Bridge (1876—78). In the foreground lies a part of the building housing the Cabinet Office, erected in 1893.

7 Prague Castle with the Cathedral of St Vitus towering high above the Theresian Palace, which dates from the second half of the 18th century. Below the palaces lie the former monastery of the Theatines and, right at the bottom, the second floor of the Lobkovicz Palace, dating from the beginning of the 18th century, from whose garden the picture was taken.

8 On the Castle rampart. From the rampart, built in 1663, there is a beautiful view of the city. From here we see, beyond the statue of St Wenceslas by Č. Vosmík (1906) Strahov with its church towers, and on the right the façade of the Schwarzenberg Palace, dating from the middle of the 16th century, the largest Renaissance building in Prague and today the Military History Museum.

9 Prague Castle seen from Petřín Hill. In the foreground, in front of the Cathedral of St Vitus, the vast building of the Theresian Palace and the Court of Honour, a building stylistically unified on the outside, which was built between 1755—77 according to the plans of the Viennese architect Nicola Pacassi. Today it houses the president's offices. Below the Castle is Úvoz (the Approach), the original way to the Castle from the town.

10 The Bohemian Coronation Jewels date from the 14th—16th centuries. The Crown of St Wenceslas was made in 1346 by order of the Emperor Charles IV, and it is

a copy of the old crown of the Přemyslids. It weighs more than four pounds, is of pure gold and contains 111 precious stones and pearls. The imperial globe and sceptre are in Renaissance style, made in the time of Rudolf II at the end of the 16th century. The globe is an exquisite example of goldsmith work. In the background is a well-known gothic panel, the votive picture of archbishop Jan Očko of Vlašim, dating from about 1370.

11, 12 The Cathedral of St Vitus in Prague Castle has two parts. The choir and belfry are the original Gothic work of the architects Matthew of Arras (1344—52) and Peter Parler and his workshop (1353—1419); the three naves and the western towers are the neo-Gothic additions of the architects J. Mocker and K. Hilbert, dating from 1873—1929. The layout of the courtyard, with its obelisk and the pedestal of the Gothic statue of St George, is by the architect Josip Plečnik and dates from 1928. Behind the obelisk is the former early Baroque Chapter House, from the second half of the 17th century. The mosaic on the Golden Gate below the belfry, depicting the Last Judgement, is from the 14th century.

13 The Cathedral of St Vitus. A view from the early 14th century choir, by Parler, looking towards the neo-Gothic nave, by Mocker, and the rose window with a glass panel by František Kysela, dating from 1921. At the bottom lies the royal tomb, the work of the Dutch sculptor Alexander Colin, made between 1563—89. The Cathedral is used for concerts of sacred music. On the triforium there is a noteworthy portrait gallery of the Luxembourgs and other personages associated with the building of the Cathedral from the 14th century.

14 The tombstone of the Czech kings, by Alexander Colin, is surrounded by lattice work by the court locksmith, Jiří Schmidthammer, dating from 1589. In the background is the Cathedral choir, work on which was begun by Matthew of Arras and, after his death, finished by Peter Parler (1352—58).

15 The interior of the Chapel of St Wenceslas. Built by Peter Parler between 1362—64, it includes the tomb of Prince Wenceslas, a reconstruction of the original tomb from the time of Charles IV. The lower part of the chapel walls is covered with precious stones, and inserted among them are paintings, representing Christ's Passion, by members of Master Theodorik's circle from 1372—73. The paintings on the upper walls represent the legend of St Wenceslas and are the work of the Master of Litoměřice, from the early 16th century. There are also portraits of King Vladislav Jagello and his wife, and below them a Gothic statue of St Wenceslas by Master Henry from the workshop of Peter Parler, dating from 1373.

16 The mosaic of the Last Judgement (1370—71) on the front wall of the Golden Gate of the Cathedral. Below the Saviour, amongst angels, kneel the patrons of Bohemia; at the bottom, in the corners, are Charles IV and his fourth wife, Elisabeth of Pomerania. The windows lead to a chamber where, guarded by seven locks, are kept the Bohemian Crown Jewels.

17 The statue of St George is a valuable bronze sculpture from the late Gothic period, from 1373. It is a work of Martin and Jiří of Kluž. In 1562 it was knocked down from its pedestal by a crush of people, but later it was repaired. In 1966 further repairs were carried out.

18 The Vladislav Hall, the largest Gothic hall in Prague, came into existence with the reconstruction of the second floor of the Old Palace of the Castle during the reign of Vladislav Jagello. The project was a work of the court architect Benedikt Rejt of Pístov. The rebuilding was carried out between 1486—1502. The windows are in Renaissance style; the vaulting is decorated with circular ribs. It is a work of B. Rejt, finished in 1502. The bronze chandeliers hanging from the vault were given to Emperor Ferdinand I by the citizens of Nuremberg around 1550. The portal in the background is of a later date; it leads to the gallery of the Chapel of All Saints. The hall, which is a kind of ante-room before the royal chambers on one side and the state and court offices on the other, was also used for tournaments, coronation banquets, and even for markets. Nowadays presidential elections take place there.

19 The ceiling of the main hall of the former burgraves at Prague Castle. It was discovered and restored during the adaptation of the burgrave's offices, a Renaissance building by the architect Giovanni Ventura dating from 1555, to form the Czechoslovak Children's House. It is one of Prague's most beautiful beam ceilings from the end of the Renaissance.

20 The President of the Republic's Office within Prague Castle. It is one of the Rococo chambers adapted, according to a design by N. Pacassi, in the 1760s.

21 The Picture Gallery within Prague Castle, created in 1964 from the remains of the Castle Gallery in the adapted stables of Ferdinand I and Rudolph II. It includes works by Tintoretto, Titian and Veronese, and a remarkable painting by young Rubens (1601) *The Gathering of the Gods.* The photograph shows the Rudolph stables, a work of the Italian architects Gargioli and Filippi, which date from about 1595.

22 Golden Lane is named after the goldsmiths who, among others, lived there in the 17th and 18th centuries. According to a legend which arose in the period of Romanticism in the 19th century, during the reign of Rudolf II alchemists lived there, who tried to produce gold and the elixir of life for the superstitious emperor. In reality the street was given to the castle guards in 1597 by Rudolph II to make their homes there. Later, other employees of the Castle moved in too. The quaint look of these parasite-like dwellings on the periphery of the Castle is in sharp contrast to the splendour of the other castle buildings. The Golden Lane is one of the curiosities of Prague.

23 The Basilica of St George is Prague's oldest standing church. Its foundation dates from about the year 920, the time of Prince Vratislav I. After the fire of 1142 it

was enlarged and rebuilt in its present form, with two towers. It was restored between 1880—1912. The side portal is early Renaissance, dating from about 1500, and comes from the workshop of Benedikt Rejt.

24 The interior of the triple-naved Basilica of St George is that of a Romanesque, Ottonian-type basilica, with a tribune adapted towards the end of the 10th century when the first convent in Bohemia was established there. The choir and crypt date from the time of the rebuilding after 1142, and bear the remains of late Romanesque wall paintings from the beginning of the 13th century.

25 The Archbishop's Palace, which stands in front of the main entrance to Prague Castle, was rebuilt in its present form by the architect J. J. Wirch in 1763—64. In the halls inside are to be found magnificent tapestries from Paris, depicting West Indian themes.

26 The Royal Summer-House, known since the 19th century as the Belvedere, is the most beautiful Renaissance building north of the Alps. It was built by Ferdinand I, according to plans by the Italian Paolo della Stella, between the years 1538—41. The upper floor was completed by Boniface Wolmut in 1563. Today it is used by the National Gallery for exhibition purposes. The bronze fountain, made between 1564—71, is a work of the foundryman Tomáš Jaroš, according to a model by the Italian Francesco Terzia.

27 The Master of Třeboň's altar-piece, *The Lowering of Christ into the Grave*, together with the other panel paintings by this artist who was one of the most progressive late Gothic painters of the second half of the 14th century, are among the most valuable paintings in the National Gallery.

28 *St John the Baptist* by Rodin. One of the casts of this famous sculpture, which dates from 1880, is exhibited in the garden of the National Gallery in Prague, which is lodged in the Sternberg Palace at Hradčany.

29 The façade of the Loreto, the oldest Marian place of pilgrimage in Bohemia. It is an extensive complex of buildings around a copy of the supposed house of the Virgin Mary at Loreto in Italy. The copy was built in 1628 and, from the second half of the 17th century onwards, was surrounded by ambits with chapels and a small church. Between 1720—22 Christoph and Kilian Dientzenhofer provided the façade of the ambit with an extensive architectural structure, including sculptures by Jan B. Kohl and Ondřej Quitainer. Above the façade is an older belfry, with chimes dating from 1694 which repeat a Marian hymn each hour.

30 The diamond monstrance from the Loreto treasure. The silver frame of the monstrance, which was made in 1699 by the Viennese goldsmiths Stegner and Känischbauer, according to a design by the architect J. B. Fischer von Erlach. It is adorned with more than 6,200 diamonds, the gift of Countess of Kolovrat.

31 This fresco from the ceiling of the Philosophy Room in the Strahov Library is a work of the Viennese painter, Anton F. Maulpertsch, dating from 1794.

32 The Strahov monastery was founded in 1140 by King Vladislav II and Bishop Jindřich Zdík for the then new Order of Premonstratensians. Over the centuries the Romanesque foundations of the church and monastery have experienced various rebuildings and adaptations, the last being the Baroque one in the latter half of the 18th century. The church dates from that time, whilst the building of the monastery next to it and the adjoining prelature have kept the sober character of their early Baroque reconstruction, which dates from the 17th century. In 1950 the monastery, for centuries a lively spiritual centre, was moved elsewhere and the Museum of Czech Literature was established in the building.

33 The Little Quarter, seen from the roof of one of the houses of Úvoz, reveals itself as a kaleidoscope of small roofs of various shapes, dating from the 17th—19th centuries, and dominated by the Church of St Nicholas. In the background is the Old Town of Prague, with the spires of the Church of Our Lady of Týn, of the Old Town Hall, the cupolas of the Church of the Knights Hospitalers and of the Church of St Saviour, the towers of Charles Bridge and of the Church of St Giles (on the right). Farther away lies Žižkov with its Trade Unions Building designed by the architects Havlíček and Honzík in 1930—32. On the left is the Memorial of Vítkov Hill, built by the architect J. Zázvorka between 1927—49, now serving as a burial place for the leaders of the Communist Party.

34 A panoramic view of Prague with Charles Bridge as a connecting link in the centre.

35 The sculpture *After the Bath* by Štursa has, since 1948, adorned a niche below the castle rampart and the side façade of the Schwarzenberg Palace.

36 Wallenstein Street showing, on the left below the towering Prague Castle, a part of the Wallenstein Palace, built by Albrecht of Wallenstein between 1623—30. On the right is the palace known originally as the Czernin Palace, later as the Kolovrat Palace, which today houses the Ministry of Culture; it is a work of the architect Palliardi and dates from about 1780. Farther on lies the Pallfy Palace, dating from the first half of the 18th century.

37 Neruda Street, which leads up to the Prague Castle, is one of the oldest thoroughfares in Prague. It is named after a famous Czech writer. The street is one of the most ancient ones in Prague; it is adorned with the Baroque façades of its houses, their gables and house signs.

38 The house sign of the house No. 233 'At the Two Suns', in Neruda Street.

39 The house sign of the house No. 210 'At the Three Little Violins' in the same street. Both date from the 18th century.

40 The Vrtba Garden in the Little Quarter (Karmelitská Street No. 25) is the most important, architecturally

and artistically, of the Baroque gardens of Prague. It is a combined work of the architect F. M. Kaňka, the sculptor M. Braun and the painter V. V. Reiner, and dates from about 1730.

41 The garden 'Na Valech', adapted in 1928 by the architect Josip Plečnik, presents one with interesting views. On the one hand, of the Old Palace of the Castle, including the wing where the historic defenestration took place — a Renaissance building instigated by Vladislav Jagello and named in honour of his son Ludvík; on the other, a panorama of the city. Beneath the Ludvík wing are memorials to the two chancellors, Slavata and Martinic, who were thrown from the windows of the first floor during the uprising of Czech nobility in 1618.

42 The Pallfy Garden on the south slope of the Castle, below the Lobkovicz Palace, is a part of the continuous enclave of Baroque gardens which was created here in the years 1710—80 on the site of old vineyards. Today these gardens provide one of the most attractive settings of old Prague.

43 The Garden of the Wallenstein Palace was constructed, together with the palace, to the order of General Albrecht of Wallenstein, between 1626—30. Architecturally it is dominated by its *Salla Terrena*, the work of the Italian builder Giovanni Pieroni, and artistically by the bronze sculptures of Adriaen de Vries (1625—26) based on themes from Greek mythology. The originals were looted as spoils of war by the Swedes in 1648, and those standing now in the garden are copies, dating from 1913—14.

44 The underside of the cupola of the Church of St Nicolas, the work of Christoph Dientzenhofer, with its fresco by F. X. Palko dating from 1735—52. The statues of the ecclesiastical fathers beneath the cupola, like all the other sculptural decorations of the church, are the work of the leading sculptor of Prague Rococo, I. F. Platzer.

45 The Church of St Nicolas in the Little Quarter, built between 1704—57, is the pride of Czech Baroque. The nave, dating from 1704—11 is a work of Christoph Dientzenhofer. The choir gallery with the cupola and belfry are a work of Kilian Ignaz Dientzenhofer and Anselmo Lurago. The church complex, including the former Jesuit College, inherited, at the time of its origin, the adjoining buildings which were structurally improved in the 18th century. The most valuable of these is the house 'At the Stone Table' in the foreground, the work of the architect J. Jäger, from 1773.

46 The belfry of the Church of St Nicolas was the crowning act in the century-long evolution of the former Jesuit residence in the Little Quarter. It was built by Anselmo Lurago in the style of radical Roman Baroque as late as 1755—57.

47 The Little Quarter Bridge Towers are the work of two periods. The lower one is Romanesque, probably dating from the 12th century and later adapted in Renaissance style, the higher is late Gothic and was built at the

expense of King Jiří of Poděbrady in 1464. The gate between them dates from the first decade of the 15th century, from the time of Václav IV.

48 The steps leading from Charles Bridge down to Kampa were built in 1844 in Neo-Gothic style. Above the stairway is the most beautiful of the Baroque sculptures on the bridge, the statue of St Lutgard by Matyáš Braun, dating from 1710.

49 A view of Kampa from Charles Bridge. Kampa is an ancient island, mentioned as early as the 12th century.

50 The public gardens on the slopes of Petřín are among the most delightful in Prague. They encompass a number of formerly private gardens that belonged to the nobility or to the Church. Their gradual opening up to the public gave the inhabitants of Prague a place of quiet recreation, and at the same time the chance to enjoy beautiful views of the ancient parts of the town. In the distance are the towers of the Old Town Hall, of the Church of Our Lady of Týn and of St James.

51 The Old Town of Prague, together with the Little Quarter, provide the largest number of old-fashioned nooks and crannies. The photograph shows the roofs, gables, corners and dormer windows of houses No. 462 and 478 on the corner of the Old Town Square and Melantrich Street.

52 The closely built-up Čertovka (Devil's) stream gives the impression of a Venetian canal, which is why this area, from Charles Bridge to the convergence of the stream with the Vltava, is indeed known as Prague's Venice.

53 Another view of Charles Bridge, the work of Parler, which was adorned between 1683—1714 with two rows of statues and sculptural compositions representing the saints, the works of such foremost masters of Baroque sculpture as Jan Brokof, Ferdinand M. Brokof, Matyáš Braun, Matyáš Jäckel and others. It has always been the most frequently visited place of interest in Prague. Until the middle of the 19th century it was the only bridge in the city and therefore the only connecting link between the right and the left bank sections. It was there where Czech coronation and funeral processions went, it was there where armies crossed the river and fought and where religious services were held. Today the bridge is closed to transport and used as a pedestrian walkway, providing beautiful views of the Castle and the Little Quarter and, on the other side of the Old Town bridge-head, of the towers and cupola of the Church of the Knights Hospitalers.

54 The Old Town Bridge Tower, dating from the 14th century, is one of the attractions of Prague, owing to the architectural progressiveness of the work of the stonemasons in Parler's workshop and, above all, to its sculptural treasures. On the bridge side these were unfortunately destroyed in 1648 during the battle between the Swedes and the burghers and soldiers of the Old Town. The Tower, the Church of the Knights Hospitalers and the façade of the Church of St Saviour, represent a breathtaking symbiosis of Gothic and

Baroque and at the same time form one of the most beautiful small squares in Europe.

55 Waterworks, baths, mills and convents occupied the bridge-head of this Prague bridge and produced a picturesque scene of verticals and horizontals. The dominant position was taken up by the Old Town waterworks — one of the oldest in Europe — the tower of which, dating from 1489 and adapted in Neo-Gothic style after the fire of 1878, serves today only as a clock tower. The waterworks building itself, rebuilt in 1883 by Wiehl, today houses the Museum of Bedřich Smetana.

56 Křižovnické Square, named after the Order of the Knights Hospitalers with a Red Star, is not large but it is a real gem of art and architecture. The order acquired the area next to the entrance to the bridge in the middle of the 13th century and gradually built a residence there, later made famous by the church, an early Baroque work by the French architect Jean B. Mathey. The cupola of the church blends harmoniously with the Gothic vertical of the Bridge Tower, which is covered with statues of Charles IV, Václav IV, and the patrons of Bohemia. It blends also with the broad North Italian-style façade of the Church of St Saviour, at one time the main church of the Jesuits in Bohemia. The church, a work of Francesco Caratti and of the sculptor Jan J. Bendl, dates from the middle of the 17th century.

57 The Old Town Bridge Tower.

58 This photograph shows the everyday look of the Old Town waterworks, mills and baths, and the tower and cupola of the Clementinum, the bastion of the Jesuit Order in Prague during the period between the middle of the 16th century and the second half of the 18th century. The tallest of the buildings is the Astronomical Tower, a work of the architect F. M. Kaňka, which dates from 1721—48.

59 The Hall of the Clementinum Library, built by Kaňka and decorated by Jan Hiebl for the Jesuits in 1727, is one of the best preserved secular interiors of Baroque Prague.

60 The rear façade of the Clementinum and the older Clam-Gallas Palace by the famous Viennese architect J. B. Fischer von Erlach, with its sculptures by Matyáš Braun dating from about 1715, compete with one another with their ostentatious, massive, Baroque forms and sculptures at the end of Husova Street.

61 The Old-New Synagogue, a reminder of the Prague Ghetto, is valued as one of the oldest structures of early Gothic Prague from the second half of the 13th century.

62 The Old Jewish Cemetery, founded in the early 15th century, served as a burial place for Prague's Jews until the end of the 18th century. It is remarkable both for the thousands of gravestones bearing the emblems of families, and for the tombs of famous personalities such as Mordechai Maizl, Rabbi Jehuda Löw ben Bezalel, Heudela Bassewi, and others.

63 The Church of St James in the Old Town was founded in the first half of the 13th century as a sanctuary of the Minorites' convent. In the 14th century the church was rebuilt in its present size; after a fire in 1689 it was renovated in Baroque style and today it offers one of the most beautiful Baroque interiors in Prague. It is also famous for the regular organ recitals held there.

64 The Old Town Square came into existence as a large market place, together with the establishment of a customs' house of the principality, a court, and a hospice for foreign traders in about the 11th century. After the founding of the town, around 1230, the market place became a square and the little Church of Our Lady of the hospice became the main parish church. As the church stood in front of a fenced-in area, it is known as the Church before the Fence (před Týnem). After 1380 it was built in its present-day form, the gable and towers being completed only in the 15th and early 16th centuries. During the Hussite period it became the metropolitan church of the Utraquist congregation of Prague. From the artistic point of view it is one of the most important monuments of Czech Gothic style. Alongside the church is the former Týn School, dating from the 13th century, which in the second half of the 16th century was given Renaissance gables; next to it, across a little street, is the house 'At the Bell', which is the best preserved Gothic house in Bohemia, dating from the first half of the 14th century.

65 Since 1338, the Old Town Hall has been a symbol of the autonomy of the town. It grew out of a private stone house with the addition of the adjoining burghers' houses. The reconstruction in the late 14th and early 15th centuries, and the addition of a 19th century building created an agglomeration which was partially destroyed in May 1945 by a fire in the main building jutting out into the square. Fortunately the most valuable parts — the tower with the chapel and the astronomical clock, the old town hall chamber and the Gothic arcades on the southern side — were preserved. The fire and demolition of the town hall by the Nazis opened up, until the town hall has been restored again, views of the ostentatiously Baroque former Parish church of St Nicholas, which had subsequently belonged to a convent. It is a work of K. I. Dientzenhofer and A. Braun, and dates from 1732—35. Except for the church in the Little Quarter dedicated to the same saint, it is the most valuable ecclesiastical Baroque building in the city.

66 Prague's astronomical clock is one of the most sought-after monuments of the city, above all because of the mobile row of wooden figures representing the Apostles, which appear each hour in its windows. The mechanism itself dates from 1410 as does the circular frame of the zodiac clock. It was only towards the end of the 15th century that the figures were added and the astronomical clock was architecturally finished in the form it bears today. The magnificent calendar panel by Josef Mánes, dating from 1865, is in a museum; the one here is a copy by the painter Čila. The façade in the background is that of the Church of Our Lady of Týn, built between the end of the 14th and 16th centuries.

67 The Carolinum was originally a private house of the master of the Mint, Rothlev, who donated it after 1370 to King Václav IV. The latter gave it to the University in 1383. The oriel chapel and vaults on the ground floor belonged to the Gothic 14th century patrician house. The Baroque architect, Kaňka, rebuilt the house in 1718, giving it the form it has today.

68 The Great Hall demonstrates the nature of the adaptation and modernization of the Carolinum, done to suit the actual needs of Charles University. The transformation of the interior has been carried out according to a design by the architect Jaroslav Fragner; the tapestry by Marie Teinitzerová reproduces a cartoon by V. Sychra; the statue of Charles IV, the founder of the university, is by Karel Pokorný.

69 The House of Artists, built between 1876—84 and designed by the architects J. Zítek and J. Schulz, was from the start dedicated to both music and the fine arts. But during the pre-war Republic the arts were moved out to make room for the National Assembly. After the war the arts, this time only the musical arts, returned in full force so that the building, one of the most valuable of Czech Neo-Renaissance achievements, is today used exclusively for concerts and the teaching of music.

70 The Tyl Theatre, originally the Nosticz or the Estates' Theatre, is the oldest theatre building in Prague. Erected by the architect A. Haffenecker between 1781—83, it became famous throughout the world as the place in which the first peformance of Mozart's *Don Giovanni* was given. The classicist building, modified in the middle of the 19th century, was renamed after the Second World War in honour of the classic Czech dramatist J. K. Tyl, and was included in the organisation of the National Theatre of Prague.

71, 72 The National Theatre is one of the buildings most sacred to the Czech people, both as a sanctuary of art and as the place of cultural manifestations in honour of Czech national sovereignty and the progressiveness of the country's national ideals. At the same time, it is one of the most beautiful of modern Czech buildings. It is a work of J. Zítek and J. Schulz, dating from 1868—83. The theatre was decorated by a whole generation of artists, the so-called Generation of the National Theatre. The outside is dominated by sculptural decorations by Bohuslav Schnirch, representing Apollo and the Muses on the attic, with bronze chariots on the pylons.

73 The National Theatre is known as The Chapel on the Vltava. The river Vltava, apart from its actual presence, is personified by a bronze sculpture with allegorical reliefs of the Vltava's four tributaries on the sides of the pedestal. The sculpture is a work of J. Pekárek.

74 Musical tradition places Prague in the forefront of world musical culture. The three happy and fruitful visits by Mozart were an important contribution to this tradition. He stayed in the Bertramka Villa, the residence of Josephine Dušek, a singer well known towards the end of the 18th century. The villa of this homestead was restored in 1956 and turned into the Mozart and Dušek Museum.

75 Not far from Bertramka lies the Cemetery of the Little Quarter, where the Dušeks are buried. The area of the cemetery, which is no longer in general use, is full of picturesque classicist and romantic memorials and tombstones dating from the end of the 18th and the beginning of the 19th centuries, creating a melancholic synthesis of man-made and natural beauty.

76 The National Museum stands at the head of the main shopping and communication artery of Prague, Wenceslas Square. The building erected by the architect J. Schulz between 1885—90 contains not only valuable collections pertaining to the evolution of nature and society in the Czech Lands, but also a Pantheon, dedicated to the memory of meritorious Czech personalities. The Pantheon constitutes the central section of the main façade of the museum, and its interior, decorated by paintings based on themes taken from Czech history, is one of the most dignified ever created in Czech neo-Renaissance style. The statue of St Wenceslas in front of the museum is by J. Myslbek.

77 Wenceslas Square, formerly the Horse Market, is the central open space of the New Town. Contemporary development of the metropolis has turned this artery, which formerly connected the gates of the Old and New Towns, into a trading centre and at the same time into the main communication hub for the whole of the city. Tall department stores and apartment houses replaced the former one- or two-storied buildings. In the second half of the 17th century a fountain with a statue of St Wenceslas was built here, which gave the market its present name. Between 1912—24 the statue was replaced by Myslbek's new monument.

78 The New Town Hall was a symbol of the autonomy of the New Town from the time of its erection in the second half of the 14th century until 1784 when a unified municipal authority was established in Prague and the Town Hall was abolished. The New Town Hall is renowned historically, as this is where in 1419 the Hussite revolutionary movement came into being, when the councillors attacked the procession of Utraquists led by Jan Želivský. At that time the building did not have its present appearance; this work dates from the middle of the 15th century (the tower) and the beginning of the 16th century (the Renaissance façade with Gothic gables). The façade was reconstructed in 1906. Inside there are notable original Gothic chambers.

79 The Powder Tower and the Municipal House of Prague. The Tower is the only remaining gate of the medieval fortifications of Prague's Old Town; it is also the youngest one. The form of architectural design and sculptural decoration was dictated by the close proximity of the Royal Court. The Tower is a work of the builder Matěj Rejsek, and dates from after 1475; but its present-day form is more or less the result of the restoration undertaken by J. Mocker between 1875—86. The Municipal House was erected between

1906—11 on the original site of the Royal Court, which had been deserted nearly five centuries earlier. In the 17th century it became a seminary, and in the 18th century barracks. In addition to the work of the architects A. Balšánek and O. Polívka, a whole series of early 20th century Czech artists contributed to the building, which was conceived in the familiar art nouveau style of Prague.

80 The New Town waterworks, which were known as the Šítka Tower after the adjacent mills, are a relic of the late Gothic building style of the 15th and 16th centuries. The site where the mills formerly stood was taken in 1930 for the building belonging to the Mánes Society of Artists, erected according to a project designed by the architect O. Novotný.

81 During the past few decades a continuous and intensive modern construction programme has been going on in Prague. This has been directed primarily towards the creation of large-scale housing estates on the perimeter of the city. Nor has the construction of public buildings been neglected; the Institute of Macromolecular Chemistry, built according to a project designed by the architect K. Prager in the Petřiny Housing Estate, belongs to the most modern style.

82, 83 Vyšehrad has been since time immemorial the second castle beneath which the settlement of Prague spread from the 10th century onwards. Around it have been woven myths, such as the one about Princess Libuše, who is supposed to have founded Prague and given rise to the dynasty of the Přemyslides. As far as this story is concerned, we know that a castle existed there in the second half of the 10th century, and that it became the seat of the ruling princes towards the end of the 11th century. In the 14th century a Gothic castle came into being, when the chapter church, dating from the end of the 11th century, was rebuilt as a Gothic cathedral. A military citadel was built there in the 17th century in place of the castle, and was in use until the 19th century. The romanticism of that century revived the legend of Vyšehrad as the place of the supposed beginnings of the Czech nation, and therefore a national burial ground was established there. Of the original buildings only the Romanesque rotunda of the cemetery of St Martin, dating from the end of the 11th century, remains.

84 The large and sparsely built-up area south of Vyšehrad was set aside for recreational purposes in recent plans for the city. In accordance with these plans, an all-year-round swimming pool, designed by the architect R. Podzemný was built there.

85 The building of Barrandov by M. Urban was an important example of the trend to turn Prague into a metropolis during the period of the first Republic. Barrandov is a rocky height above the Vltava, named in memory of a French paleonthologist who made large fossil finds there in the first half of the 19th century. Apart from film studios, the building complex also includes a large comfortable restaurant and a swimming pool at the foot of the cliff.

86 The view from Barrandov over the housing estate at Lhotka reveals the character of the new housing estates that are being built in Prague.

87 The Castle Rampart was built in 1663 and the adjoining little Church of the Virgin Mary of Einsiedeln in 1672—73. The platform in front of it, adorned by a pillar with a statue of the Virgin, is a much sought-after viewpoint from which to view the panorama of Prague.

PLATES

1 Prague panorama with the Vltava islands, seen from Jirásek Bridge

2 Kampa Island, with the Castle and Petřín Hill

3 The Castle and the Little Quarter seen from the Smetana Embankmer

4 Prague panorama seen from
the Petřín look-out tower

5 The Castle and the Little Quarter seen from Charles Bridge

6 Prague bridges seen from Letná Hill

7 Prague Castle viewed from the Lobkovicz Palace garden

8 The Strahov monastery and the Schwarzenberg Palace, seen from the Castle rampart

10 The coronation jewels of the Kingdom of Bohemia

9 The Castle seen from Petřín Hill

12 The Cathedral of St Vitus; view of the north façade

14 The Cathedral Choir, with the royal tomb

15 The interior of the St Wenceslas Chapel in the Cathedral

13 The interior of the Cathedral

16 The mosaic of the Golden Gate of the Cathedral

17 The statue of St George and the Obelisk in the Third Castle Courtyard

18 Vladislav Hall in the Old Palace of the Castle

19 The ceiling of the main hall of the former burgraves at the Castle

20 The President of the Republic's Office in the Castle

21 The Picture Gallery in Prague Castle

22 Golden Lane

23 The Basilica of St George

24 The interior of the Basilica of St George

25 The Archbishop's Palace at Hradčany

26 The Royal Summer-House (Belvedere) and the Singing Fountain

27 The Master of Třeboň, '*The Lowering of Christ into the Grave*', in the National Gallery

28 A cast of Rodin's statue, '*St John the Baptist*', in the National Gallery

29 The façade of the Loreto at Hradčany   30 The diamond monstrance in the Loreto

31 A. Maulpertsch's fresco on the ceiling of the Strahov Library   32 The Strahov monastery, now the Museum of Czech Literature

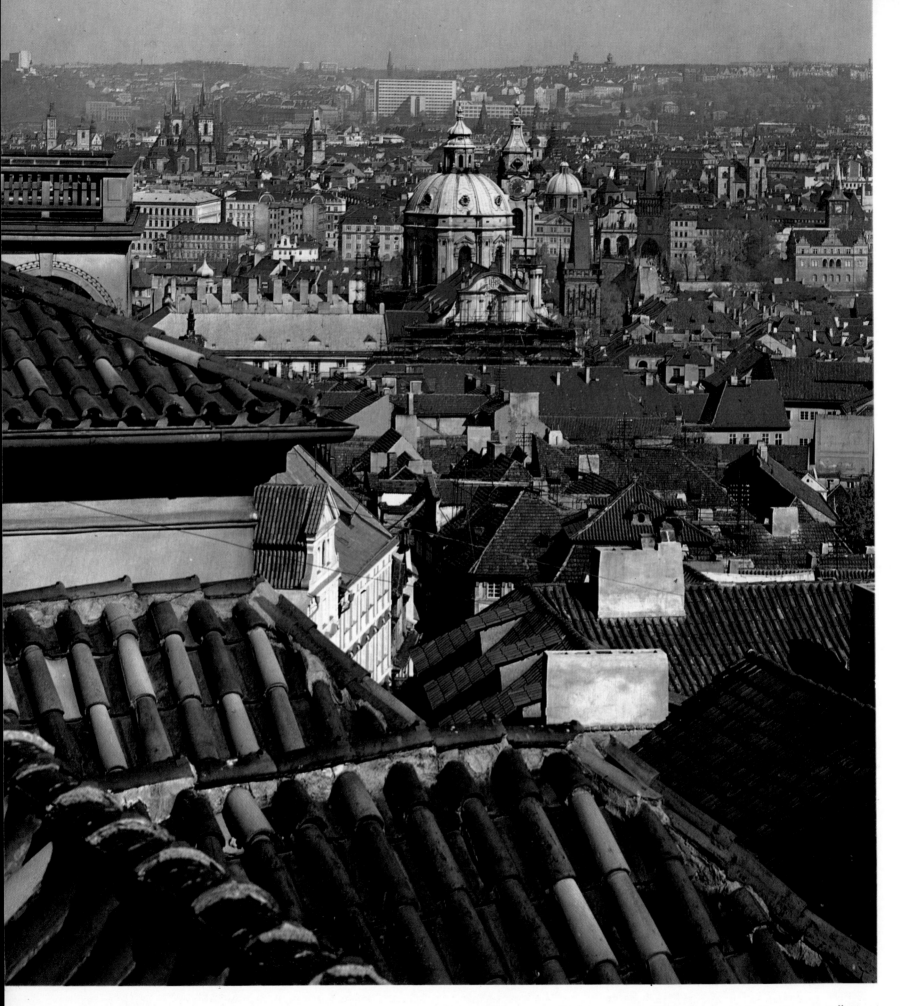

33 The Little Quarter and the Old Town; in the background Žižkov

34 Panoramic view of Prague with Charles Bridge

35 J. Štursa's '*After the Bath*' in Neruda Street in the Little Quarter

36 Wallenstein Street in the Little Quarter

37 Neruda Street in the Little Quarter

38 The house sign 'At the Two Suns' in Neruda Street

39 The house sign 'At the Three Little Violins' in Neruda Street

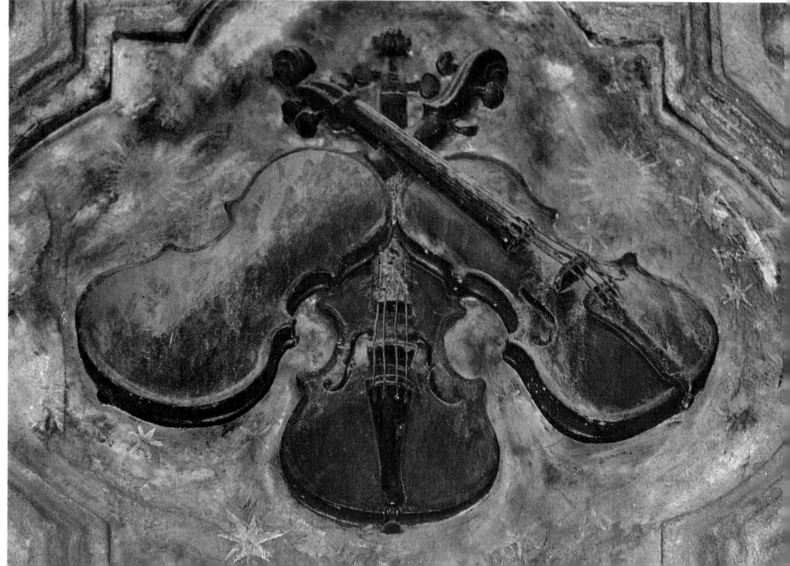

41 The garden 'Na Valech' at Prague Castle

40 The Vrtba Garden in the Little Quarter

43 The *Salla Terrena* of the Wallenstein Palace in the Little Quarter

44 The interior of the Church of St Nicolas in the Little Quarter

45 The Church of St Nicolas, illuminated for ceremonial occasions

47 The Little Quarter Bridge Towers festively illuminated

46 The belfry of the Church of St Nicolas

48 The steps from Charles Bridge down to Kampa

49 Idyll on Kampa Island

50 In the Seminary Garden on the slopes of Petřín

51 View over the roofs of Melantrich Street in the Old Town

54 The Old Town Bridge Tower
    and the Church
    of the Knights Hospitalers

55 Nocturne on the Vltava
    by the Smetana Museum

56 The Churches of the Knights
   Hospitalers and of St Saviour
   in the Old Town

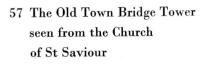

57 The Old Town Bridge Tower
   seen from the Church
   of St Saviour

58 The Old Town waterworks
and the old mills

59 The Library Hall of the Clementinum   60 The Clementinum and the Clam-Gallas Palace in the Old Town

**61 The Old-New
Synagogue**

62 The Old Jewish Cemetery

64 The Church of Our Lady of Týn in the Old Town

63 The Church of St James in the Old Town

65 The Old Town Hall and the Old Town Church of St Nicolas   66 The Clock Tower and the Church of Our Lady of Týn

68 The Great Hall of the Carolinum

67 The Carolinum

69 The House of Artists, or Rudolfinum, in the Old Town

70 The Tyl Theatre in the Old Town

71 The Chariots on the
   National Theatre

72 The National Theatre

73 The Vltava Monument, the National Theatre, and Shooters' Island

74 The Bertramka Villa in Smíchov

75 The Little Quarter Cemetery

76 The National Museum in the New Town

77 Wenceslas Square

78 The New Town Hall on Charles Square

79 The Powder Tower and the Municipal House of Prague

81 The Macromolecular Chemistry Institute at Petřiny

80 The New Town waterworks and the Mánes Society building

82 Vyšehrad

83 The Church of St Martin at Vyšehrad

84 The swimming pool at Podolí

85 Barrandov and its restaurant and swimming pool

86 Bráník and the housing estate at Lhotka

87 Petřín Hill seen from the ramparts of Prague Castle ▶